Inside the NFL

Oakland Raiders

BY
ZACH WYNER

AV² provides enriched content that supplements and complements this book. Weigl's AV² books strive to create inspired learning and engage young minds in a total learning experience.

Your AV² Media Enhanced books come alive with...

Audio
Listen to sections of the book read aloud.

Key Words
Study vocabulary, and complete a matching word activity.

Video
Watch informative video clips.

Quizzes
Test your knowledge.

Go to **www.av2books.com**, and enter this book's unique code.

BOOK CODE

J819910

Embedded Weblinks
Gain additional information for research.

Slide Show
View images and captions, and prepare a presentation.

AV² by Weigl brings you media enhanced books that support active learning.

Try This!
Complete activities and hands-on experiments.

... and much, much more!

Published by AV² by Weigl
350 5th Avenue, 59th Floor
New York, NY 10118
Websites: www.av2books.com   www.weigl.com

Library of Congress Control Number: 2014930850

ISBN 978-1-4896-0870-3 (hardcover)
ISBN 978-1-4896-0872-7 (single-user eBook)
ISBN 978-1-4896-0873-4 (multi-user eBook)

Printed in the United States of America in North Mankato, Minnesota
1 2 3 4 5 6 7 8 9 0   18 17 16 15 14

042014
WEP150314

Project Coordinator Aaron Carr
Art Director Terry Paulhus

Photo Credits
Every reasonable effort has been made to trace ownership and to obtain permission to reprint copyright material. The publishers would be pleased to have any errors or omissions brought to their attention so that they may be corrected in subsequent printings.

Weigl acknowledges Getty Images as its primary image supplier for this title.

Oakland Raiders

CONTENTS

Introduction

The Raiders are one of the most often discussed and written about teams in the National Football League (NFL). The history of the Raiders is made up of more stories and characters than just about any team in professional sports. From the dominant **Super Bowl** winning teams of the 1970s and 1980s, to their former owner Al Davis, to the silver and black uniforms, the Raiders are a franchise that cannot be forgotten.

The Raiders have played in two California cities, Oakland and Los Angeles. Beginning in Oakland in 1960, local fans were heartbroken when the team moved 350 miles (560 kilometers) south to Los Angeles in 1982.

Despite a few stumbles in the past few years, the Raiders have won 54 percent of their games played.

For many of the fans, however, distance did not matter. As members of Raider Nation, the trip was a small sacrifice to make in order to support their team. In 1995, the Raiders moved back to Oakland. Since then, hundreds of members of Raider Nation have driven north eight Sundays per year to support their team.

Darren McFadden has been the starting running back for the Raiders since 2008.

Stadium O.co Coliseum

Division American Football Conference (AFC) West

Head coach Dennis Allen

Location Oakland, California

Super Bowl titles 1976, 1980, 1983

Nicknames The Silver and Black, The Men in Black, The Team of the Decades, The Nation, America's Most Wanted, Raider Nation

21
Playoff Appearances

3
Super Bowl Championships

15
Division Championships

History

WINNING STREAK

After reaching the playoffs for the first time in 1967, the Raiders went on a remarkable run. Over the next 18 years, the team reached the playoffs 15 times and won four championships.

Marcus Allen was the first player in NFL history to gain more than 10,000 career rushing yards and 5,000 career receiving yards.

The Oakland Raiders were one of eight teams to take part in the **American Football League's (AFL)** first season of 1960. Three years later, they hired Al Davis to be their coach and **general manager**. At 33 years old, Davis was the youngest person in NFL history to hold either position. Al Davis oversaw the transformation of the Raiders. Davis had his team play an aggressive **West Coast offense**, changed the uniforms to silver and black, and coined the various slogans, such as "Just Win, Baby," that gave the team an identity. In 1967, John Rauch, who came after Davis, coached the Raiders to an AFL Championship. However, it was not until the arrival of coach John Madden in 1969 that the Raiders reached a level of consistent success. Madden's Raiders won seven division titles, nine playoff games, and Super Bowl XI.

In 1978, Tom Flores became the head coach and led the Raiders to Super Bowl victories in two different cities. Players like Jim Plunkett, Lester Hayes, Ted Hendricks, and Marcus Allen led the Raiders to their second Super Bowl title in 1980. Despite their unsettling 1982 move to Los Angeles, the team went out and won another Super Bowl in 1983. In 1995, owner Al Davis moved the Raiders back to Oakland. Led by NFL **most valuable player (MVP)** Rich Gannon, and legendary receivers Jerry Rice and Tim Brown, the Raiders won three straight division titles from 2000 to 2002, and one AFC Championship.

John Madden's 130 wins as the Raiders' head coach are the most in franchise history. Madden's mark is 20 more than the next closest coach, Tom Flores.

The Stadium

O.co Coliseum holds 63,123 fans.

The Raiders moved several times in their early years, from San Francisco's Kezar Stadium, to Candlestick Park, to Frank Youell Field, before finally landing at the O.co Coliseum. Then, after spending 16 years settling in, they moved to Los Angeles. For 15 years, the Oakland community felt the team's absence. The O.co Coliseum was still home to the Oakland Athletics baseball team, but the Raiders' disappearance left a hole that baseball just could not fill. In 1995, the Raiders returned, and Raider Nation and O.co Coliseum welcomed them home.

The Raiders fans are known for a "Commitment to Excellence" both in their strong support of their team and with their outrageous outfits in the stands.

Today, O.co Coliseum is the only professional sports facility to serve both a Major League Baseball and an NFL team. It is also unique in that the playing surface is 21 feet (6.4 meters) below sea level. Its sunken playing field makes it look like a short stadium from the outside, but in fact it is quite large. O.co Coliseum has featured many events throughout the years. In addition to hosting Major League Soccer games, it is a popular venue for the world's biggest musical acts.

Members of Raider Nation head to Ribs and Things for tender pork ribs with tangy barbecue sauce.

Where They Play

CANADA

Washington

30

Oregon

Montana

North Dakota

Minnesota

Lake Superior

23

Wisconsin

Idaho

South Dakota

22

29

Wyoming

Nebraska

Iowa

24

15

Nevada

Utah

14

13

Illinois

California

Colorado

Kansas

Missouri

UNITED STATES

31

16

Arizona

New Mexico

Oklahoma

Arkansas

Mississippi

32

17

Texas

Louisiana

Pacific Ocean

12

Alaska

Hawai'i

MEXICO

27

Gulf of Mexico

0 500 Miles
0 500 km

0 100 Miles
0 100 km

AMERICAN FOOTBALL CONFERENCE

EAST		NORTH		SOUTH		WEST	
1	Gillette Stadium	5	FirstEnergy Stadium	9	EverBank Field	13	Arrowhead Stadium
2	MetLife Stadium	6	Heinz Field	10	LP Field	14	Sports Authority Field at Mile High
3	Ralph Wilson Stadium	7	M&T Bank Stadium	11	Lucas Oil Stadium	15	O.co Coliseum
4	Sun Life Stadium	8	Paul Brown Stadium	12	NRG Stadium	16	Qualcomm Stadium

O.CO COLISEUM™

Location
7000 Coliseum Way
Oakland, CA 94621

Broke ground
April 15, 1964

Completed
September 18, 1966

Surface
bluegrass

Features
- 6,300 club seats
- variable seating capacity
- easy access to BART (Bay Area Rapid Transit)

LEGEND
- American Football Conference
- National Football Conference
- ☆ O.co Coliseum

Lake Michigan
Lake Huron
Lake Ontario
Lake Erie

Michigan
New Hampshire
Vermont
Maine
New York
Massachusetts
Rhode Island
Connecticut
Pennsylvania
New Jersey
Delaware
Maryland
Ohio
Indiana
West Virginia
Virginia
Kentucky
Tennessee
North Carolina
South Carolina
Georgia
Alabama
Florida

Atlantic Ocean

0 — 250 Miles
0 — 250 Kilometers

NATIONAL FOOTBALL CONFERENCE

EAST		NORTH		SOUTH		WEST	
17	AT&T Stadium	21	Ford Field	25	Bank of America Stadium	29	Levi's Stadium
18	FedExField	22	Lambeau Field	26	Georgia Dome	30	CenturyLink Field
19	Lincoln Financial Field	23	Mall of America Field	27	Mercedes-Benz Superdome	31	Edward Jones Dome
20	MetLife Stadium	24	Soldier Field	28	Raymond James Stadium	32	University of Phoenix Stadium

The Uniforms

ADIOS, SEÑORS

The Oakland Raiders were named the **OAKLAND SEÑORS** for NINE DAYS after the team was founded in 1959. However, the community laughed at the name, and the team went in a with a different name.

The Raiders have only worn their white jerseys at home once in their history. This was during a 2008 game against the San Diego Chargers.

The Raiders have perhaps the single most memorable uniform in all of sports. Their silver and black colors have given them an identity since Al Davis designed the uniforms in the mid-1960s, replacing the original black, gold, uniforms with no **logo**. Today, members of Raider Nation throughout the country proudly display their devotion by wearing the silver and black every Sunday.

HOME

Since first appearing in 1963, the Raiders' uniforms have gone through only minor changes. Black jerseys have silver numbers while white jerseys have black numbers with a silver outline. All jerseys are paired with silver pants with a black stripe down the side.

AWAY

The Raiders wore black cleats as a tribute to Al Davis during the 2012 and 2013 seasons. The team plans to continue this tradition.

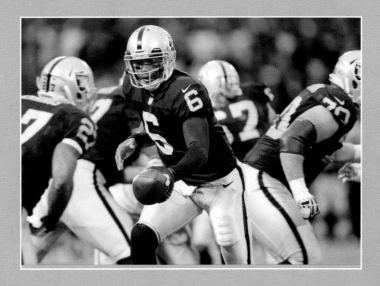

The Helmets

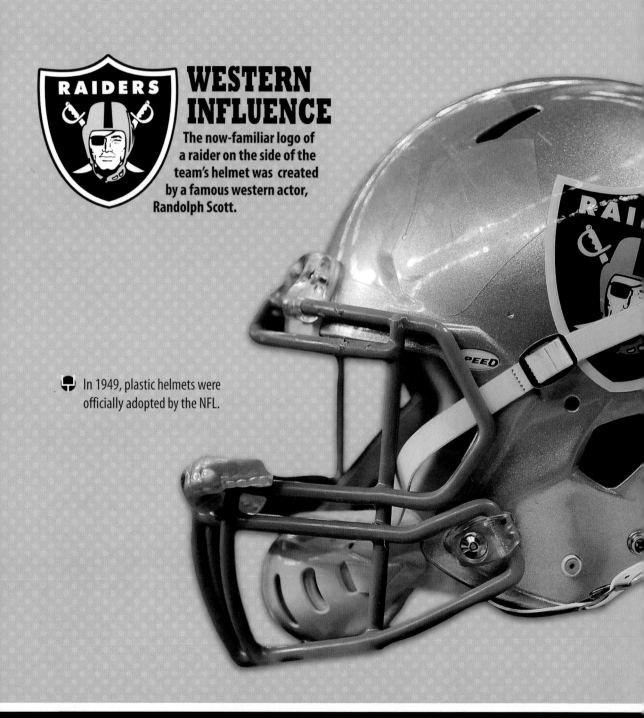

WESTERN INFLUENCE

The now-familiar logo of a raider on the side of the team's helmet was created by a famous western actor, Randolph Scott.

In 1949, plastic helmets were officially adopted by the NFL.

Similar to the uniforms, the Raiders' helmets have not changed much since 1963. During the franchise's first three years, when the uniforms were black and gold, the helmet was black with a white stripe down the center and no logo. When Al Davis arrived, he changed the helmet color to silver and added the now iconic logo.

Desiring a logo that would fit the tough-as-nails reputation that Davis wanted to create, the Raiders settled on logo that would come to be as well known as any logo in professional sports. It is a black shield with a pair of silver, crossed swords, and a helmeted Raider wearing an eye patch. Since 1964, the logo has gone unchanged.

Spearing is when a defensive player makes contact with an offensive player with the crown of his helmet. This act results in a 15 yard penalty.

The Coaches

10 From 1995 to today, the Raiders have employed 10 different head coaches, with no coach lasting longer than four years.

4 Like Al Davis and John Madden before him, Dennis Allen got his first job as a head coach before turning 40.

The Oakland Raiders' identity was created through the words and actions of their head coaches. Coach, general manager, and owner Al Davis coined many mottoes that defined what it meant to be a member of the franchise, including "Commitment to Excellence," and "Once a Raider, Always a Raider." Every head coach since has tried to live up to the level of commitment that Davis showed.

JOHN MADDEN

At the age of 32, John Madden took the job of head coach in 1969. In just 10 seasons, he coached the Raiders to 103 regular-season wins and a Super Bowl title. When asked about Madden, owner Al Davis said, "One of his great virtues, the fire that burned brightest in him, was his love and passion for football, which was seldom ever equaled."

TOM FLORES

Tom Flores is one of just two people to win a championship as a player, assistant coach, and head coach, and he was the first minority coach to win a Super Bowl. After taking over for John Madden in 1979, Flores guided the Raiders to two Super Bowl Championships in nine years.

DENNIS ALLEN

In 2012, the Raiders hired the 39-year-old to be the 18th head coach of the franchise. While Allen's Raiders have struggled through his first two seasons, the team remains hopeful that the defensive-minded Allen will turn things around in 2014.

Team Spirit

In 2009, Ice Cube recorded a song titled "Raider Nation" to recognize the passion of Raiders fans everywhere.

For many years, the Raiders felt no need for a mascot. Over the years, the Black Hole has been a place where fans have felt free to express their inner Raider by wearing crazy costumes. These costumes have ranged from a gorilla, to skeletons in Raiders' uniforms, to a Raider-loving Darth Vader. In 2013, however, the Raiders had a new mascot that fans of Nickelodeon's TV show *NFL Rush Zone* quickly recognized.

Raiders fans are known for arriving early, dressing up, and for bringing the noise on game days.

The Oakland Raiders' new official mascot is named Raider Rusher. He has a giant Raider head, a spiked helmet, and a pair of legs where his neck might otherwise be. On game day, Raider Rusher appears in a section of the stadium called Raiderville, as well as the three kids zones located inside O.co Coliseum.

If you happen to sit in sections 104 to 107 of the O.co Coliseum, you are officially in the Black Hole and among the most rowdy Raider fans.

Legends of the Past

Many great players have suited up in the Raiders silver and black. A few of them have become icons of the team and the city it represents.

Howie Long

For 13 seasons in the silver and black, Howie Long terrorized opposing quarterbacks. Using an uppercut move called the "rip," Long broke through the grip of offensive lineman, and used his quickness and strength to get into the **backfield**.

An eight-time **Pro Bowler**, Long registered double-digit **sacks** each season from 1983 to 1985. He was also a first-team **All-Pro** each of those three seasons. The biggest game of Long's career came in Super Bowl XVIII, when he helped the Raiders stifle a powerful Washington Redskins running game to win their third Super Bowl Championship.

Position Defensive End
Seasons 13 (1981–1993)
Born January 6, 1960, in Charlestown, Massachusetts

Marcus Allen

Position Running Back
Seasons 16 (1982–1997)
Born March 26, 1960, in San Diego, California

The Los Angeles Raiders selected Marcus Allen in the 1982 **NFL Draft**, gaining the explosiveness and speed that their running game lacked. As a senior at the University of Southern California, Allen had won the **Heisman Trophy** after rushing for 2,342 yards. He was the first running back in college football history to run for more than 2,000 yards in a single season.

In Allen's second NFL season, he led the Super Bowl-champion Raiders in rushing and was third on the team in receiving yards. His receiving skills helped him lead the NFL in **yards from scrimmage** twice during his Pro Football **Hall of Fame** career.

Ken Stabler

Known as much for his legs in his early years as for his throwing strength, Ken Stabler changed his style of play in the mid-1970s. The victim of severe knee injuries, Stabler came to rely on his accurate passing and hall of fame receiving targets, wide receiver Fred Biletnikoff and tight end Fred Casper. Stabler's finest season came in 1976. He led the league in completion percentage (66.7), passing touchdowns (27), and quarterback rating (103.4), was named the AFC's Player of the Year, and guided the Raiders to a 32-14 Super Bowl win over the Minnesota Vikings.

Position Quarterback
Seasons 15 (1970–1984)
Born December 25, 1945, in Foley, Alabama

Tim Brown

In the 1987 NFL Draft, the Raiders selected Tim Brown with the sixth overall pick. Having just become the first wide receiver in college football history to win the Heisman Trophy, Brown was seen as a future NFL star. Gifted with fast speed and superior field vision, he was a threat as punt returner as well as a wide receiver. It did not take long for him to realize his potential. In Brown's rookie season, he led the NFL with 2,317 all-purpose yards. In 16 years as a Raider, he made nine Pro Bowls and registered 1,000-plus receiving yards in nine-straight seasons.

Position Wide Receiver
Seasons 17 (1988–2004)
Born June 22, 1966, in Dallas, Texas

Stars of Today

Today's Raiders team is made up of many young, talented players who have proven that they are among the best players in the league.

Justin Tuck

After starting only two games during the 2007 season, Justin Tuck starred on the world's biggest stage. In Super Bowl XLII against the undefeated New England Patriots, Tuck lived in the backfield, recording two sacks and a forced fumble. When Michael Strahan retired, Justin Tuck took his place as a starter on the defensive line. The next season, Tuck made his first Pro-Bowl. In Super Bowl XLVI, Tuck again terrorized Tom Brady and the Patriots, recording two more sacks and leading the New York Giants to their second title in four years. During his nine seasons in New York, Tuck made two Pro Bowls and recorded 60.5 sacks before becoming an Oakland Raider in 2014.

Position Defensive End
Seasons 9 (2005–2013)
Born March 29, 1983, in Kellyton, Alabama

Darren McFadden

Owing to injuries, Darren McFadden has yet to realize his potential. It is a moment that Raider Nation eagerly awaits. When healthy, McFadden has used his great speed and firm grip to be one of the best Raider running backs since Marcus Allen. In 2010, his most productive season in the Silver and Black, McFadden gained 1,664 yards from scrimmage in just 12 games and scored 10 touchdowns. As the Raiders enter the 2014 season, they hope that McFadden will be on the field, and healthy, as the team tries to reverse their fortunes.

Position Running Back
Seasons 6 (2008–2013)
Born August 27, 1987, in North Little Rock, Arkansas

Charles Woodson

I n 1997, Charles Woodson led the Michigan Wolverines to a national title and became the first primarily defensive player ever to win the Heisman Trophy. In 1998, while playing with the Raiders, he took home Defensive Rookie of the Year honors. After eight seasons with the Raiders, Woodson began playing for the Green Bay Packers. On May 21, 2013, after seven seasons in Green Bay, the eight-time Pro Bowler, seven-time All-Pro, and 2009 Defensive Player of the Year returned to Oakland.

Position Cornerback/Free Safety
Seasons 16 (1998–2013)
Born October 7, 1976, in Sebring, Ohio

Sebastian Janikowski

S ebastian Janikowski is one of the most valuable players in the National Football League. Using his powerful 6-foot, 1-inch, 260-pound frame, Janikowski is capable of making field goals that other kickers would not even consider trying. Yet, while Janikowski regularly attempts long field goals, he is remarkably accurate. In 2012, he made 31 of 34 attempts, including six from 50 or more yards. Janikowski owns NFL records for the longest field goal made in overtime (57 yards), the most field goals of 60 or more yards in a career (2), and the most field goals of 50 or more yards in a single game (3).

Position Kicker
Seasons 14 (2000–2013)
Born March 2, 1978, in Walbrzych, Poland

All-Time Records

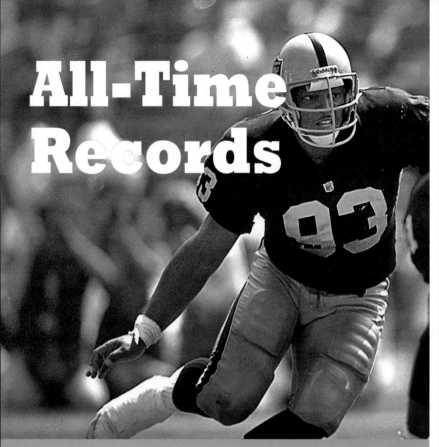

107.5 Career Sacks

For 12 seasons, defensive lineman Greg Townsend tormented offenses, setting a club record for sacks in the process.

14,734 Career Receiving Yards

In 14 seasons with the Raiders, Tim Brown had more than 1,000 receiving yards in a season nine times.

8,545 Career Rushing Yards

Marcus Allen holds the Raiders' all-time mark for rushing yards and yards from scrimmage (12,803).

19,078
Career Passing Yards

In 10 seasons with the Raiders, Ken Stabler won a Super Bowl and set the Raiders' all-time passing mark.

103 Career Wins

In just 10 seasons, John Madden coached the Raiders to 103 regular-season wins and a **winning percentage** of .763.

Timeline

Throughout the team's history, the Oakland Raiders have had many memorable events that have become defining moments for the team and its fans.

1969
The Raiders hire John Madden as their new head coach. In Madden's first season, quarterback Daryle Lamonica has a career year, guiding the Raiders to their third straight division title and a playoff victory. The season ends in disappointment, as the Raiders lose the AFL Championship Game for the second year in a row.

January 30, 1960
Months before the AFL's **inaugural** season, the Los Angeles Chargers' owner threatens to give up his team unless another AFL team is placed on the West Coast. The city of Oakland is awarded the eighth and final AFL franchise.

On January 22, 1984, Super Bowl XVIII MVP Marcus Allen rushes for 191 yards on 20 carries and the Raiders win their third NFL championship.

| 1960 | 1965 | 1970 | 1975 | 1980 | 1985 |

January 25, 1981
After playoff wins against Houston, Cleveland, and San Diego, the Raiders face the Philadelphia Eagles' NFL-best defense in Super Bowl XV. Plunkett completes 13 of 21 passes for 261 yards and three touchdowns as the Raiders win their second Super Bowl title.

1963
After three terrible seasons, the team hires 33-year-old Al Davis to be their head coach and general manager. Davis introduces a pass-heavy offense. In his first season, the Raiders go 10-4 but narrowly miss the playoffs. Davis is named the AFL Coach of the Year.

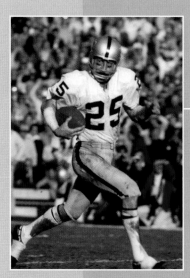

January 9, 1977
After several promising seasons that ended in disappointment, the Raiders finally win a league title. They defeat the Minnesota Vikings, 32-14, gaining a then-Super Bowl record 429 yards. Fred Biletnikoff is named Super Bowl MVP.

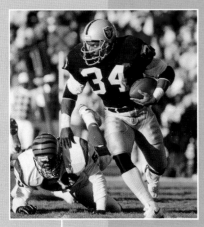

The Future
Following their last trip to the Super Bowl, the Raiders have had a rough decade. Owner Al Davis died in 2011. Meanwhile, the franchise has yet to establish a new identity in his absence. In 2014, head coach Dennis Allen's Raiders will attempt to change all of that and rise to the top of a tough AFC West.

1990
Under the NFL's first African American head coach Art Shell, the Raiders win their first division title since 1985. Star Raider running back Bo Jackson suffers a devastating leg injury during a playoff game and is forced to retire from football.

In 2001, hall of famers Jerry Rice and Tim Brown combine for more than 2,300 receiving yards and Oakland wins another AFC West crown.

| 1990 | 1995 | 2000 | 2005 | 2010 | 2015 |

In 1995, the Raiders return to Oakland and are greeted by their faithful Bay Area fans.

2002
Rich Gannon, the 2002 NFL MVP, leads the Raiders to their third straight division title and an AFC Championship. In Super Bowl XXXVII, the Raiders face Tampa Bay and former coach Jon Gruden. Gruden's familiarity with the Raiders' offense spells disaster for Oakland, as Tampa Bay intercepts Gannon five times.

2012
The Raiders replace head coach Hue Jackson with Dennis Allen, hoping that Allen's reputation as a defensive genius is well-earned.

Write a Biography

Life Story

A person's life story can be the subject of a book. This kind of book is called a biography. Biographies often describe the lives of people who have achieved great success. These people may be alive today, or they may have lived many years ago. Reading a biography can help you learn more about a great person.

Get the Facts

Use this book, and research in the library and on the Internet, to find out more about your favorite Raider. Learn as much about this player as you can. What position does he play? What are his statistics in important categories? Has he set any records? Also, be sure to write down key events in the person's life. What was his childhood like? What has he accomplished off the field? Is there anything else that makes this person special or unusual?

Use the Concept Web

A concept web is a useful research tool. Read the questions in the concept web on the following page. Answer the questions in your notebook. Your answers will help you write a biography.

Concept Web

Your Opinion
- What did you learn from the books you read in your research?
- Would you suggest these books to others?
- Was anything missing from these books?

Adulthood
- Where does this individual currently reside?
- Does he or she have a family?

Childhood
- Where and when was this person born?
- Describe his or her parents, siblings, and friends.
- Did this person grow up in unusual circumstances?

Write a Biography

Accomplishments off the Field
- What is this person's life's work?
- Has he or she received awards or recognition for accomplishments?
- How have this person's accomplishments served others?

Help and Obstacles
- Did this individual have a positive attitude?
- Did he or she receive help from others?
- Did this person have a mentor?
- Did this person face any hardships?
- If so, how were the hardships overcome?

Accomplishments on the Field
- What records does this person hold?
- What key games and plays have defined his or her career?
- What are his or her stats in categories important to his or her position?

Work and Preparation
- What was this person's education?
- What was his or her work experience?
- How does this person work; what is the process he or she uses?

Trivia Time

Take this quiz to test your knowledge of the Oakland Raiders.
The answers are printed upside-down under each question.

1 Which Raider was named NFL MVP in 2002?

A. Rich Gannon

2 Which Raiders head coach led them to their first Super Bowl win?

A. John Madden

3 How many Super Bowls have the Raiders won in their history?

A. Three

4 Which Raiders head coach was the NFL's first African American head coach?

A. Art Shell

5 Who changed the Raiders' colors to silver and black?

A. Al Davis

6 Which Raiders running back was named MVP of Super Bowl XVIII?

A. Marcus Allen

7 Which future Hall of Fame defensive back returned to the Raiders in 2013?

A. Charles Woodson

8 In what year did the Raiders return to Oakland from Los Angeles?

A. 1995

9 Which head coach did the Raiders hire in 2012?

A. Dennis Allen

10 Which player is the Raiders' all-time sacks leader?

A. Greg Townsend

Key Words

All-Pro: an NFL player judged to be the best in his position for a given season

American Football League (AFL): a major American Professional Football league that operated from 1960 until 1969, when it merged with the National Football League (NFL)

backfield: the area of play behind either the offensive or defensive line

general manager: the team executive responsible for acquiring the rights to player personnel, negotiating their contracts, and reassigning or dismissing players no longer desired on the team

hall of fame: a group of persons judged to be outstanding in a particular sport

Heisman Trophy: an annual award given to the college football player who best demonstrates excellence and hard work

inaugural: marking the beginning of an institution, activity, or period of office

logo: a symbol that stands for a team or organization

most valuable player (MVP): the player judged to be most valuable to his team's success

NFL Draft: an annual event where the NFL chooses college football players to be new team members

Pro Bowler: NFL player who takes part in the annual all-star game that pits the best players in the National Football Conference against the best players in the American Football Conference

sacks: a sack occurs when the quarterback is tackled behind the line of scrimmage before he can throw a forward pass

Super Bowl: the NFL's annual championship game between the winning team from the NFC and the winning team from the AFC

West Coast offense: the offensive system popularized by Bill Walsh, characterized by short, horizontal passing routes used to "stretch out" defenses, opening up the potential for long runs or long passes

winning percentage: the number of games won divided by the total number of games played; a coach with 7 wins in 10 games would have a winning percentage of 70 percent

yards from scrimmage: the total of rushing yards and receiving yards from the yard-line on the field from which the play starts

Index

Log on to www.av2books.com

AV² by Weigl brings you media enhanced books that support active learning. Go to www.av2books.com, and enter the special code found on page 2 of this book. You will gain access to enriched and enhanced content that supplements and complements this book. Content includes video, audio, weblinks, quizzes, a slide show, and activities.

AV² Online Navigation

Audio
Listen to sections of the book read aloud

Book Pages
AV² pages directly correspond to pages in the book.

Video
Watch informative video clips.

Key Words
Study vocabulary, and complete a matching word activity.

Embedded Weblinks
Gain additional information for research.

Try This!
Complete activities and hands-on experiments.

Quizzes
Test your knowledge.

Slide Show
View images and captions, and prepare a presentation.

AV² was built to bridge the gap between print and digital. We encourage you to tell us what you like and what you want to see in the future.

Sign up to be an AV² Ambassador at www.av2books.com/ambassador.